THE PLATINUM COLLECTION

GEORGE GERSHWIN

50 classic songs for piano and voice with guitar chords

© 2006 by Faber Music Ltd
First published in 2006 by Faber Music Ltd
Bloomsbury House 74–77 Great Russell Street London WC1B 3DA
Cover by Lydia Merrills-Ashcroft
Introduction and compilation by Jack Long
Music processed by Donald Sheppard
Printed in England by Caligraving Ltd
All rights reserved

ISBN10: 0-571-52684-5
EAN13: 978-0-571-52684-0

To buy Faber Music publications or to find out about the full range of titles available
please contact your local retailer or Faber Music sales enquiries:

Faber Music Limited, Burnt Mill, Elizabeth Way, Harlow, CM20 2HX England
Tel: +44 (0)1279 82 89 82   Fax: +44 (0)1279 82 89 83
sales@fabermusic.com   fabermusic.com

CONTENTS

INTRODUCTION

Like so many songwriters of the early twentieth century – both composers and lyricists – George Gershwin was born to Russian-Jewish parents who had emigrated to the United States of America in search of a better life. We don't know when he changed his original first name (Jacob) to George, but we do know that his family name (Gershowitz) was altered as a result of his admiration for the comedian Ed Wynn and that, as George became famous, the rest of the family were happy to adopt this new form.

As a result of his older brother, Ira, being presented with a piano, George discovered an ability to play the instrument which very quickly overtook that of anyone else in the family. Soon afterwards he began studying with a brilliant teacher, Charles Hambitzer, who introduced him to the world of classical music, both ancient and modern. Ungifted at anything else, however, he left school at fifteen and became Tin Pan Alley's youngest-ever 'song-plugger', joining the publishing firm of Jerome K Remick at $15.00 a week. Naturally enough, he was soon turning out songs of his own. One of these, 'Swanee' (written at the age of nineteen), was picked up by Al Jolson and became a huge hit worldwide – the biggest, as it turned out, of his entire career.

It sounds like a typical showbiz cliché to say that fame and fortune immediately followed, but this is exactly what happened. Together with his brother, Ira, who now joined him as his principal lyricist, George Gershwin became the name most closely associated with American popular music throughout the 1920s and for most of the 1930s – until 1937, in fact, when, tragically, at the age of only 38, he died from an undiagnosed brain tumour. The great success enjoyed by the many revues and musical comedies bearing his name becomes obvious when you look at the titles of the songs contained in this volume: they are all equally well-known and equally brilliant.

Although it isn't, of course, just the songs for which he is remembered. Concert pieces like *Rhapsody in Blue* and *An American in Paris*, as well as the equally outstanding Piano Concerto in F will form an essential part of our rich orchestral repertoire for as long as 20th century music is played. (Incidentally, and to illustrate Gershwin's 'common' touch, that famous clarinet glissando at the beginning of *Rhapsody in Blue* was played as a joke during rehearsal by the principal clarinettist; and, although it wasn't part of the Ferde Grofé orchestration – Gershwin had scored the piece for an ensemble much smaller than the full Paul Whiteman Orchestra – the composer liked it so much he incorporated it into the score.)

But, as much as we love those big crashing chords in the Rhapsody and the car horns in *An American in Paris*, it's the timeless melodies and simple, honest sentiments of the wonderful songs that we associate with George Gershwin. And here they all are, the very best of them, collected together in one volume for you to play and enjoy for years to come.

A FOGGY DAY

Music and Lyrics by George Gershwin and Ira Gershwin

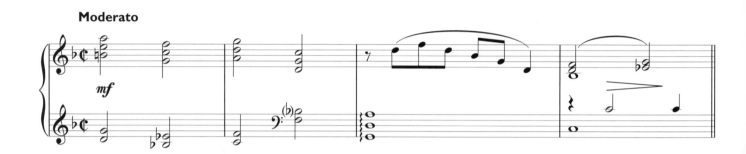

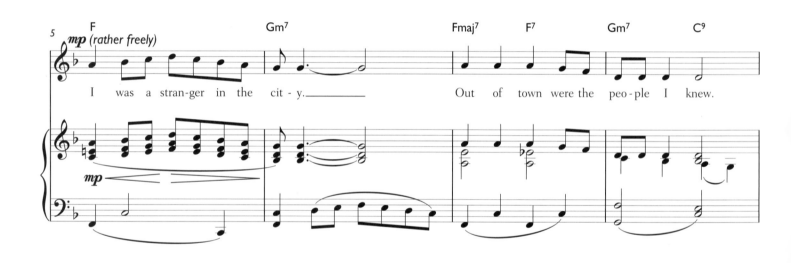

I was a stran-ger in the cit - y. Out of town were the peo-ple I knew.

I had that feel-ing of self - pi - ty, What to do? What to do? What to do? The

BESS, YOU IS MY WOMAN
from *Porgy And Bess*

Music and Lyrics by George Gershwin, Du Bose and Dorothy Heyward and Ira Gershwin

12

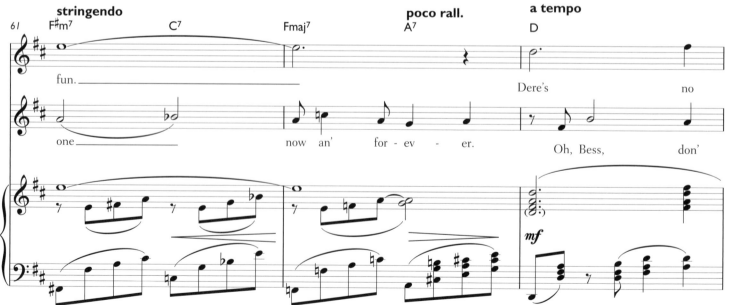

BUT NOT FOR ME

from *Girl Crazy*

Music and Lyrics by George Gershwin and Ira Gershwin

Old Man Sun-shine lis-ten, you! Nev-er tell me, "Dreams come true!" Just

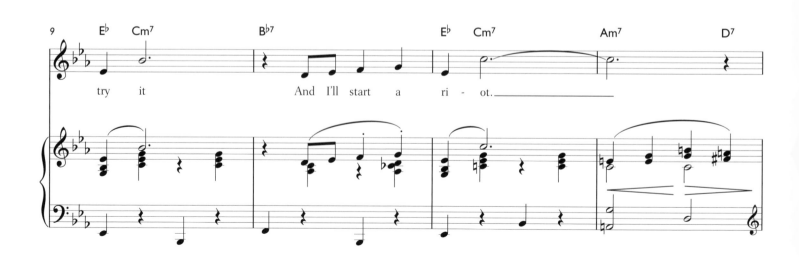

try it And I'll start a ri - ot. Just

CLAP YO' HANDS

from *Oh, Kay!*

Music and Lyrics by George Gershwin and Ira Gershwin

Come on, you chil - dren, gath - er a - round,

Gath - er a - round, you chil - dren___ And we will lose that e - vil spir - it called the

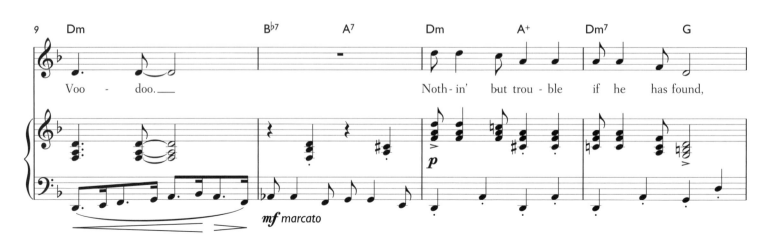

Voo - doo.___ Noth - in' but trou - ble if he has found,

DO IT AGAIN

from *The French Doll*

Words by Buddy De Sylva
Music by George Gershwin

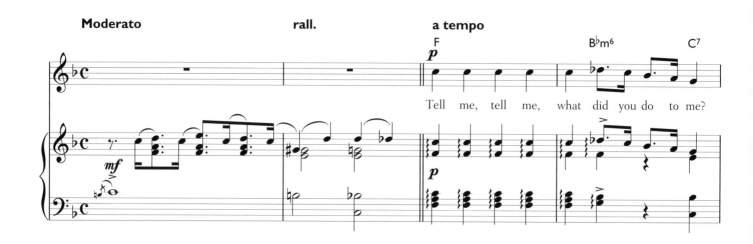

Tell me, tell me, what did you do to me?

I just got a thrill that was new to me, When your

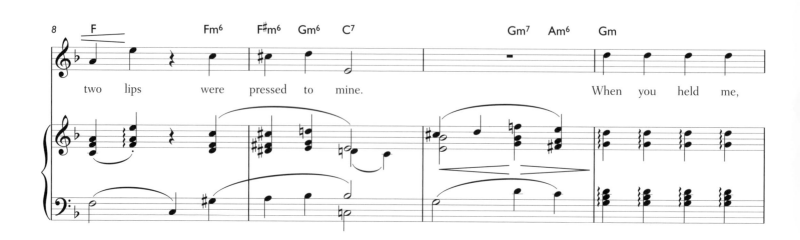

two lips were pressed to mine. When you held me,

DO, DO, DO

from *Oh, Kay!*

Music and Lyrics by George Gershwin and Ira Gershwin

EMBRACEABLE YOU

from *Girl Crazy*

Music and Lyrics by George Gershwin and Ira Gershwin

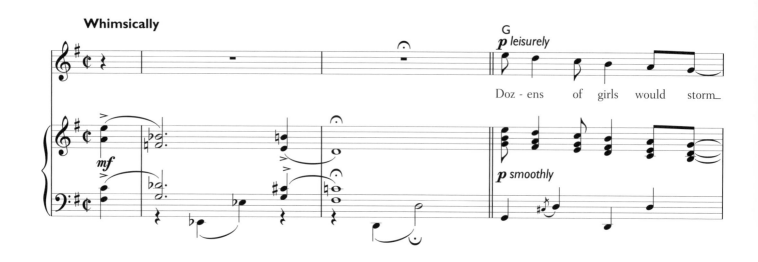

FASCINATING RHYTHM

from *Lady, Be Good!*

Music and Lyrics by George Gershwin and Ira Gershwin

FIDGETY FEET
from *Oh, Kay!*

Music and Lyrics by George Gershwin and Ira Gershwin

42

THE BABBITT AND THE BROMIDE
from *Funny Face*

Music and Lyrics by George Gershwin and Ira Gershwin

FUNNY FACE

from *Funny Face*

Music and Lyrics by George Gershwin and Ira Gershwin

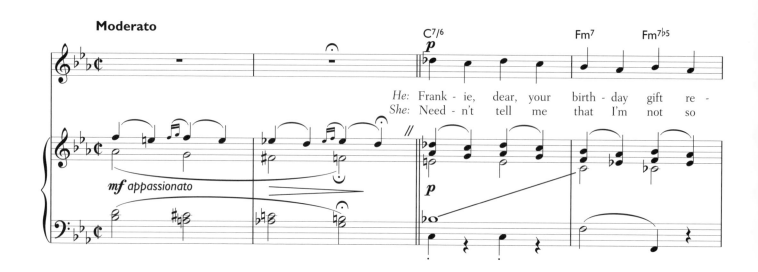

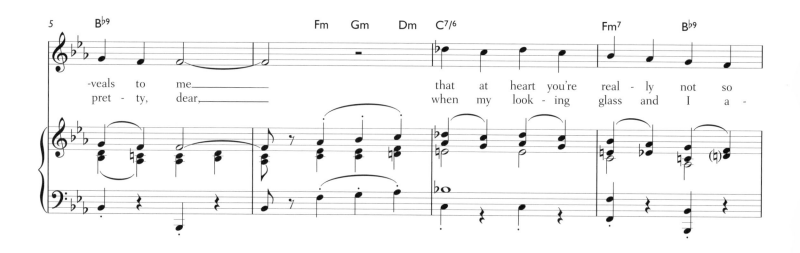

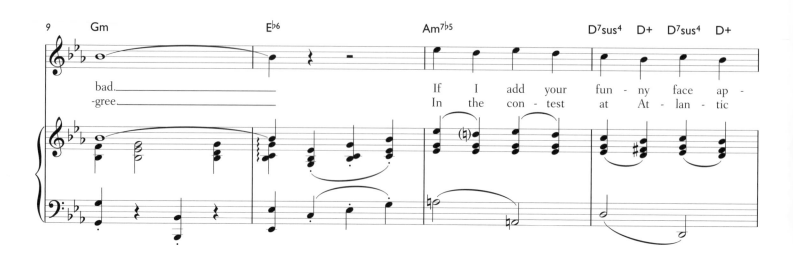

HE LOVES AND SHE LOVES

from *Funny Face*

Music and Lyrics by George Gershwin and Ira Gershwin

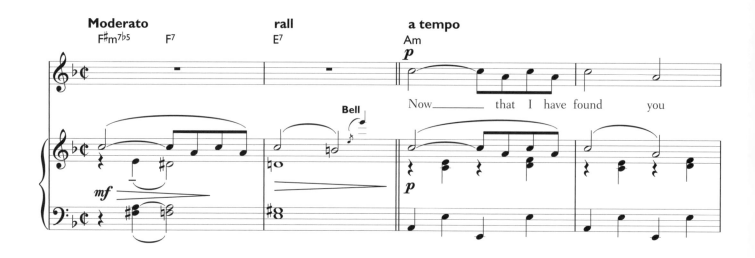

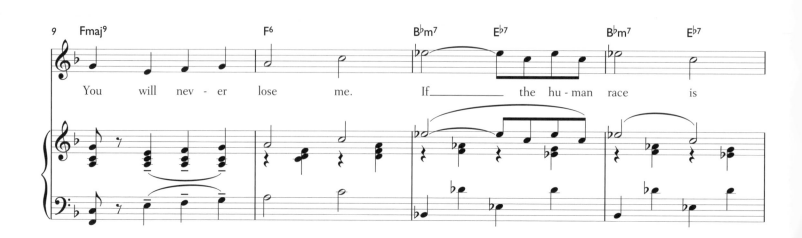

HIGH HAT

from *Funny Face*

Music and Lyrics by George Gershwin and Ira Gershwin

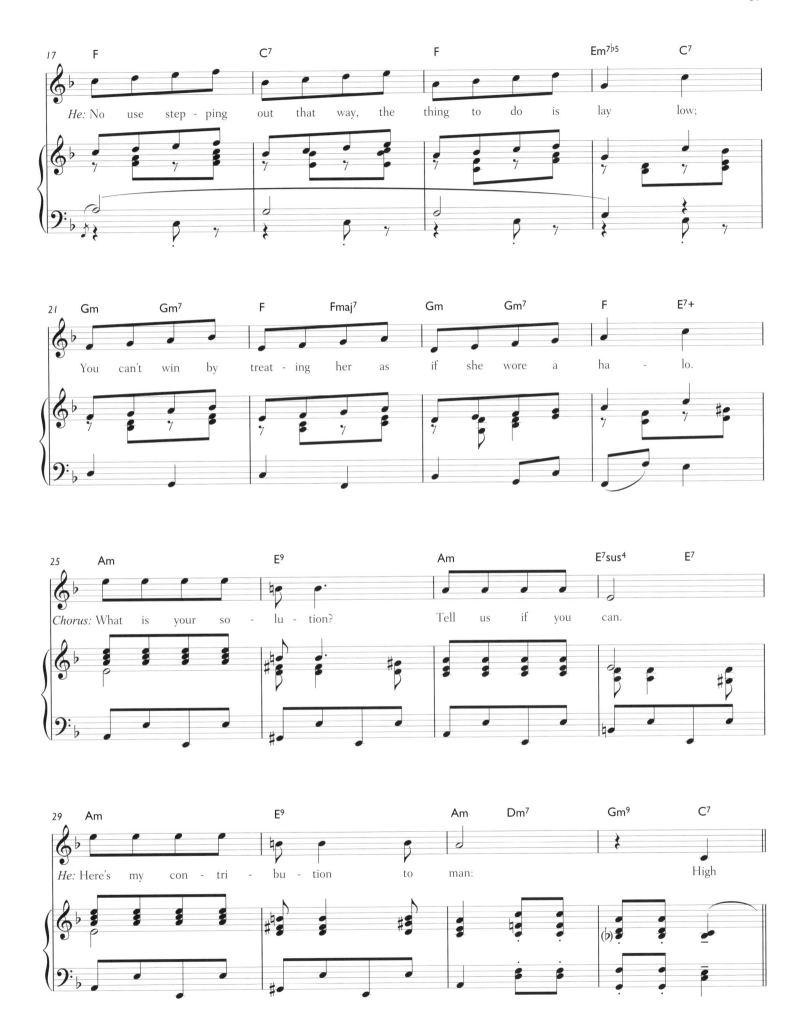

HOW LONG HAS THIS BEEN GOING ON?

Music and Lyrics by George Gershwin and Ira Gershwin

He: As a tot, when I trot-ted in lit-tle vel-vet pant - ies,_____
She: 'Neath the stars at ba-zaars of-ten I've had to ca-ress men,_____

I was kissed by my sis-ters, my cous-ins and my aunt - ies._____
Five or ten dol-lars then I'd col-lect from all those yes men._____

Sad to tell, it was Hell, an in-fer-no worse than Dan - te's._____
Don't be sad, I must add that they meant no more than chess - men._____

I GOT PLENTY O' NUTTIN'

from *Porgy And Bess*

Music and Lyrics by George Gershwin, Du Bose and Dorothy Heyward and Ira Gershwin

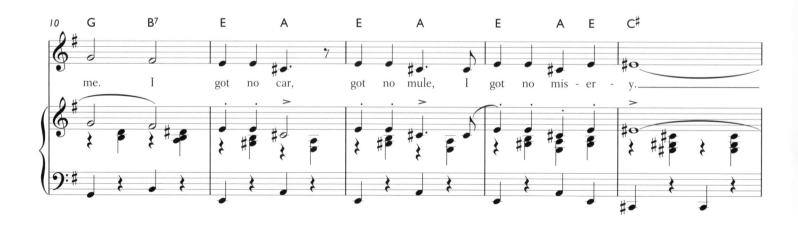

I GOT RHYTHM

from *Girl Crazy*

Music and Lyrics by George Gershwin and Ira Gershwin

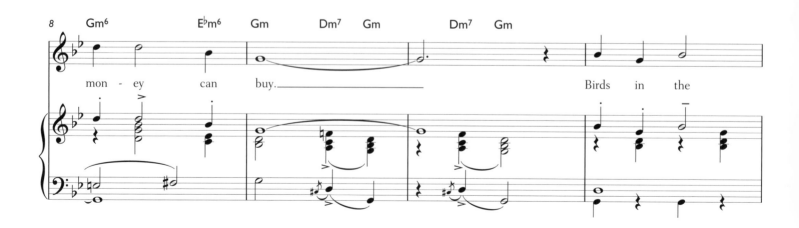

I'LL BUILD A STAIRWAY TO PARADISE

from *George White's Scandals Of 1922*

Words by Buddy DeSylva and Ira Gershwin
Music by George Gershwin

1. All you Preach - ers Who de-light in pan-ning the
2. Ev - 'ry new step Helps a bit; but an - y old

dan - cing teach - ers, Let me tell you there are a lot of fea - tures
kind of two - step Does as well. It don't mat - ter what step you step,

77

I'VE GOT A CRUSH ON YOU

from *Strike Up The Band*

Music and Lyrics by George Gershwin and Ira Gershwin

Allegretto giocoso (gaily)

He: How
She: How

glad the man-y mil-lions of An-na-belles and Lill-ians would be_____
glad a mil-lion lad-dies from mil-lion-aires to cad-dies would be_____

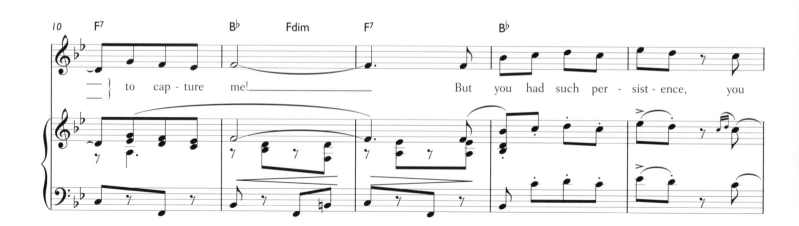

to cap-ture me!_____ But you had such per-sist-ence, you

wore down my re - sist - ance: I fell,_____ and it was swell._____

She: You're my big and brave and hand - some Ro - me - o. How I

won you I shall nev - er, nev - er know. *He:* It's not that you're at - tract - ive, But

oh my heart grew ac - tive when you_____ came in - to view._____

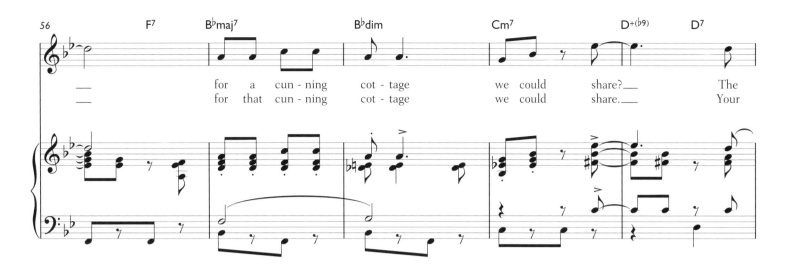

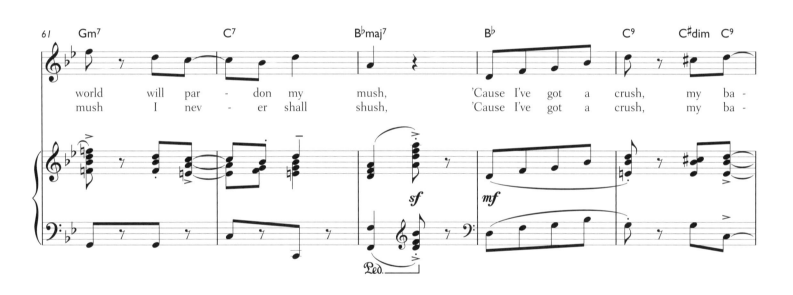

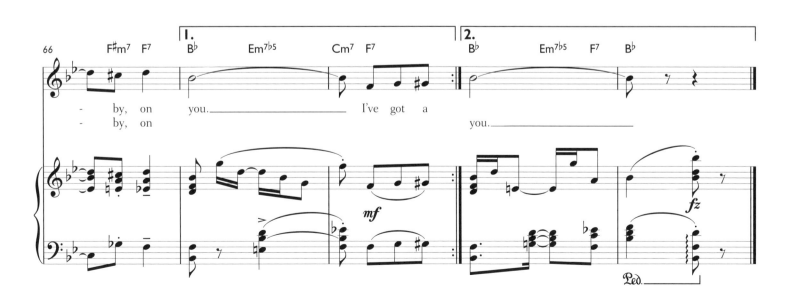

IT AIN'T NECESSARILY SO
from *Porgy And Bess*

Music and Lyrics by George Gershwin, Du Bose and Dorothy Heyward and Ira Gershwin

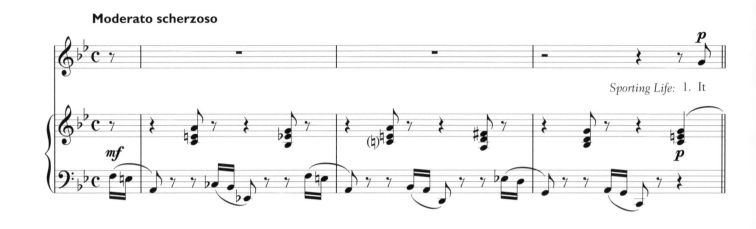

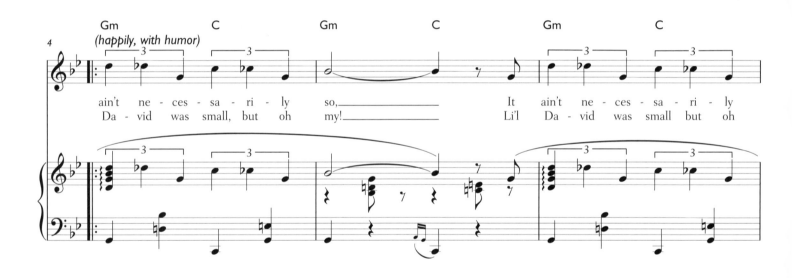

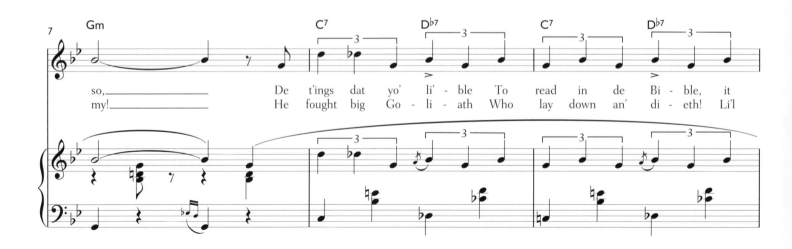

LET'S KISS AND MAKE UP

from *Funny Face*

Music and Lyrics by George Gershwin and Ira Gershwin
Arranged by Jack Gibbons

LOVE IS HERE TO STAY

from *The Goldwyn Follies*

Music and Lyrics by George Gershwin and Ira Gershwin

The more I read the pa - pers The less I com - pre - hend The

world and all its ca - pers And how it all will end. Noth - ing seems to be

LOVE IS SWEEPING THE COUNTRY
from *Of Thee I Sing*

Music and Lyrics by George Gershwin and Ira Gershwin

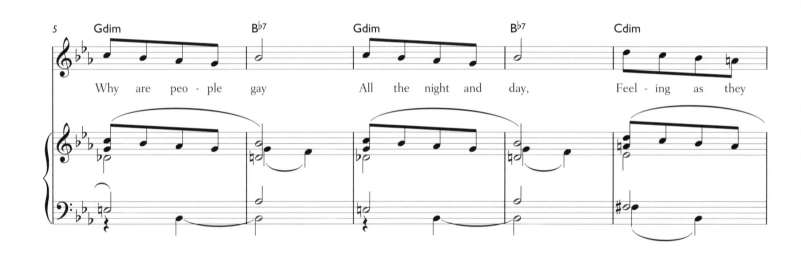

LOVE WALKED IN
from *The Goldwyn Follies*

Music and Lyrics by George Gershwin and Ira Gershwin

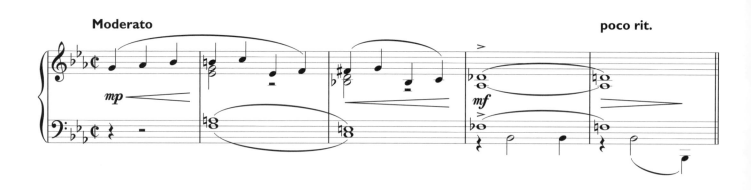

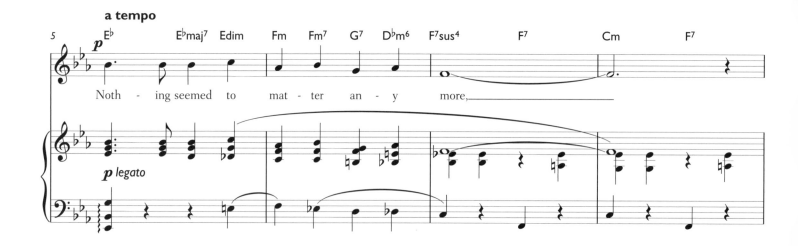

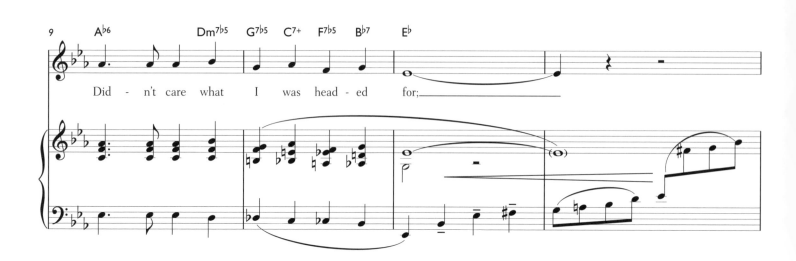

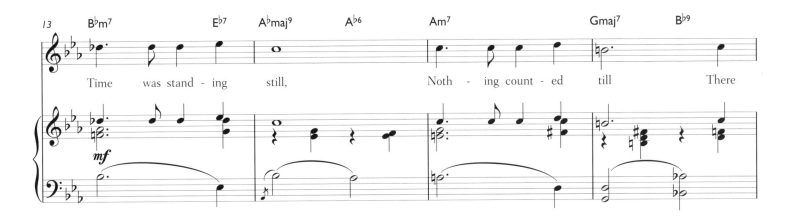

Slowly, with much expression

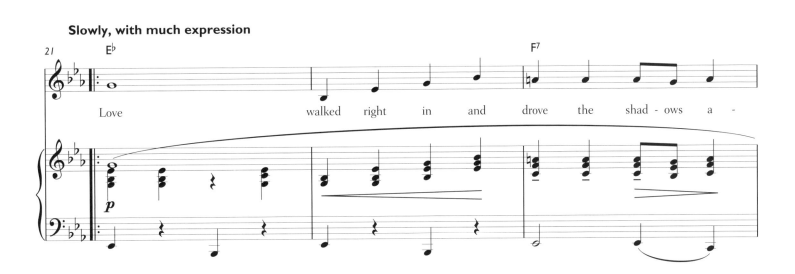

THE MAN I LOVE

from *Lady, Be Good!*

Music and Lyrics by George Gershwin and Ira Gershwin

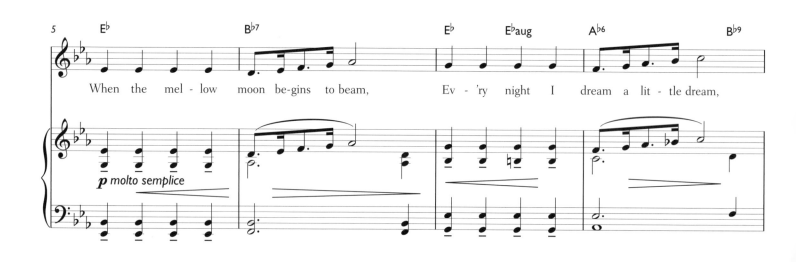

When the mel - low moon be - gins to beam, Ev - 'ry night I dream a lit - tle dream,

And of course Prince Charm - ing is the theme, The he for me. Al -

MAYBE

Music and Lyrics by George Gershwin and Ira Gershwin

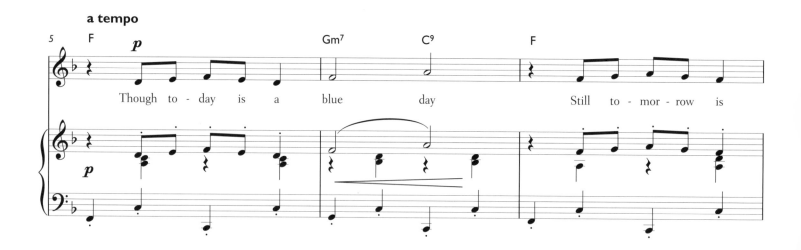

Though to-day is a blue day Still to-mor-row is

near, And per-haps with the new day

110

MY ONE AND ONLY (WHAT AM I GONNA DO)

from *Funny Face*

Music and Lyrics by George Gershwin and Ira Gershwin

114

NICE WORK IF YOU CAN GET IT

from *Damsel In Distress*

Music and Lyrics by George Gershwin and Ira Gershwin

Moderato

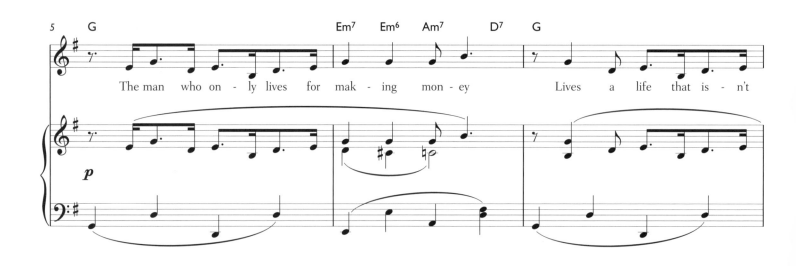

The man who on - ly lives for mak - ing mon - ey Lives a life that is - n't

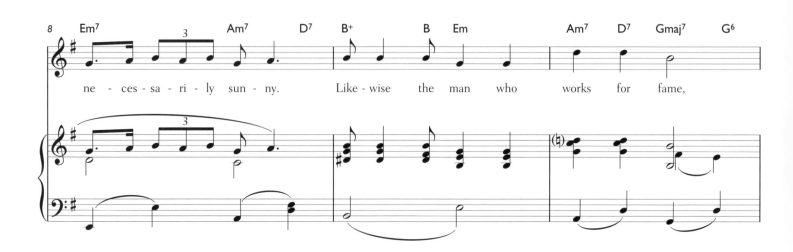

ne - ces - sa - ri - ly sun - ny. Like - wise the man who works for fame,

OF THEE I SING (BABY)

from *Of Thee I Sing*

Music and Lyrics by George Gershwin and Ira Gershwin

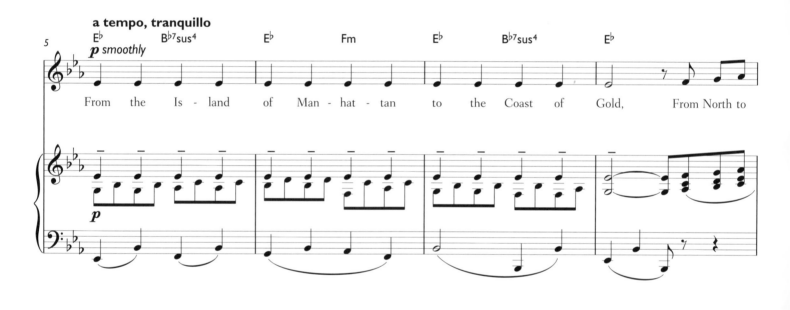

122

OH, KAY!

from *Oh, Kay!*

Lyrics by Ira Gershwin and Howard Dietz
Music by George Gershwin

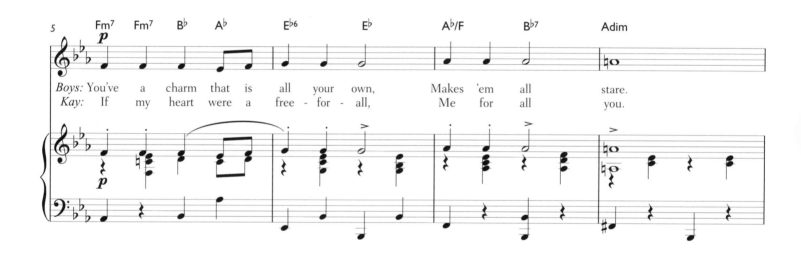

Boys: You've a charm that is all your own, Makes 'em all stare.
Kay: If my heart were a free-for-all, Me for all you.

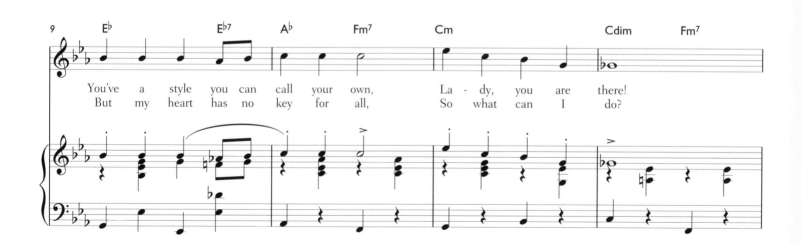

You've a style you can call your own, La-dy, you are there!
But my heart has no key for all, So what can I do?

ROSALIE
from *Rosalie*
Music and Lyrics by George Gershwin and Ira Gershwin

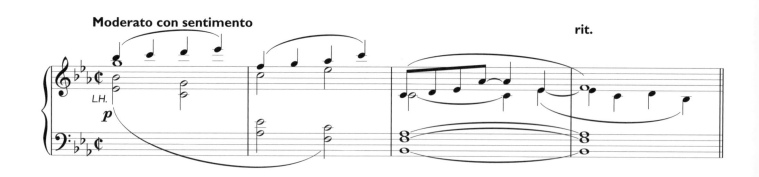

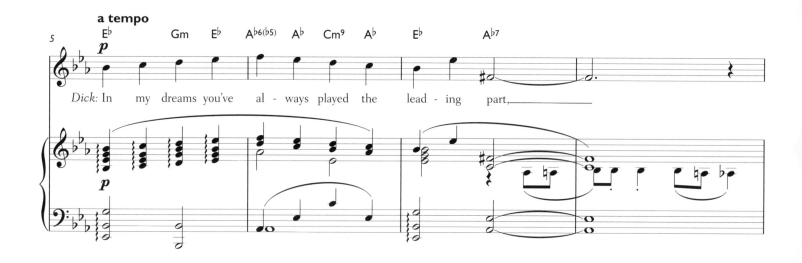

Dick: In my dreams you've al- ways played the lead- ing part,

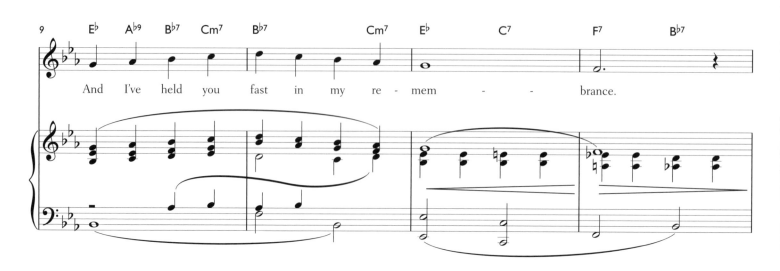

And I've held you fast in my re- mem - - brance.

'S WONDERFUL
from *Funny Face*

Music and Lyrics by George Gershwin and Ira Gershwin

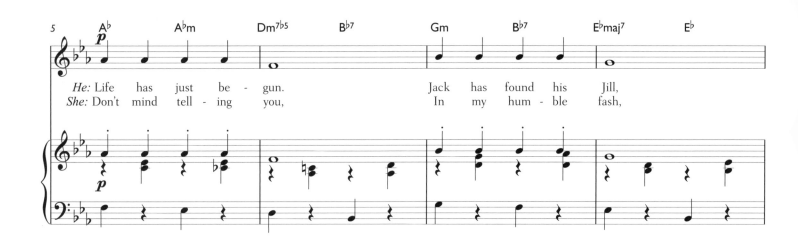

He: Life has just be - gun. Jack has found his Jill,
She: Don't mind tell - ing you, In my hum - ble fash,

Don't know what you've done, But I'm all a - thrill.
That you thrill me through With a ten - der pash.

134

SOMEBODY LOVES ME
from *George White's Scandals Of 1924*

Words by Buddy DeSylva and Ballard MacDonald
Music by George Gershwin

Warner/Chappell North America, London W6 8BS and Redwood Music Ltd (Carlin), London NW1 8BD

138

SOMEONE TO WATCH OVER ME

from *Oh, Kay!*

Music and Lyrics by George Gershwin and Ira Gershwin

There's a say - ing old Says that love is blind, Still we're of - ten told, "Seek and

ye shall find." So I'm going to seek A cer - tain lad I've had in mind.

STRIKE UP THE BAND

from *Strike Up The Band*

Music and Lyrics by George Gershwin and Ira Gershwin

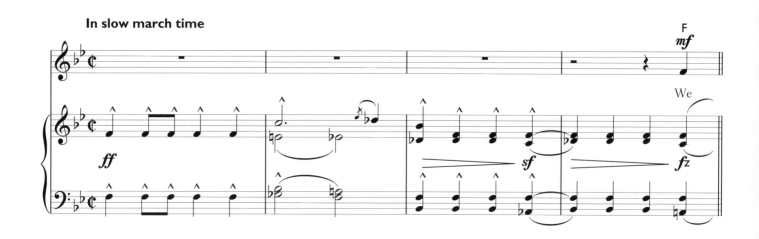

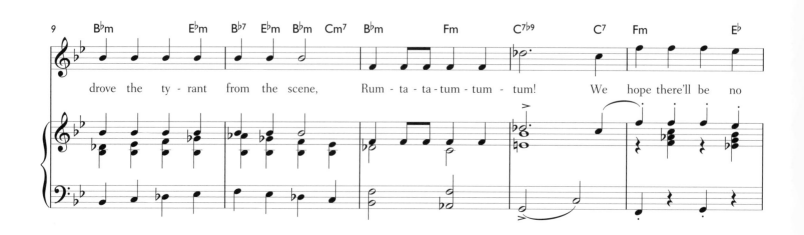

146

SWEET AND LOW-DOWN
from *Tip-Toes*

Music and Lyrics by George Gershwin and Ira Gershwin

THEY CAN'T TAKE THAT AWAY FROM ME

from *Shall We Dance?*

Music and Lyrics by George Gershwin and Ira Gershwin

Our ro - mance won't end on a sor - row - ful note, Though by to - mor - row you're

gone;___ The song is end - ed, but as the song-writ - er wrote, The

155

THINGS ARE LOOKING UP
from *Damsel In Distress*

Music and Lyrics by George Gershwin and Ira Gershwin

157

WHO CARES? (SO LONG AS YOU CARE FOR ME)

from *Of Thee I Sing*

Music and Lyrics by George Gershwin and Ira Gershwin

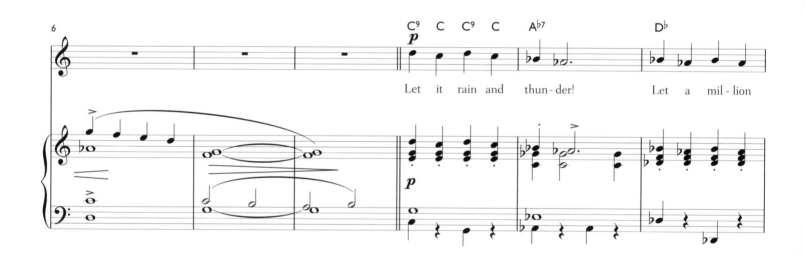

ISN'T IT A PITY?

from *Pardon My English*

Music and Lyrics by George Gershwin and Ira Gershwin

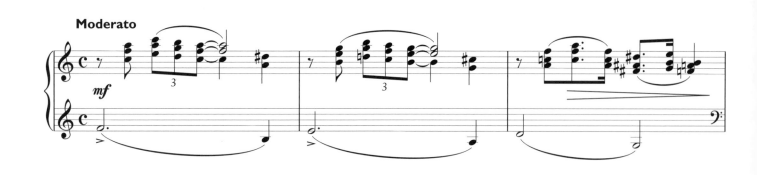

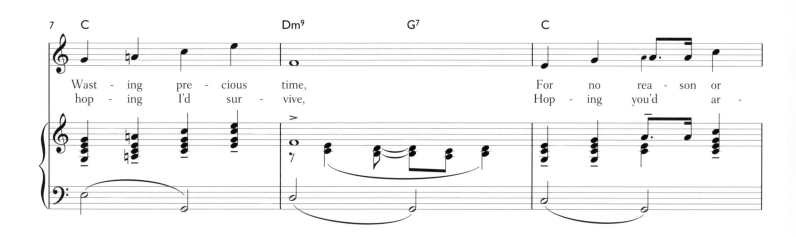

BIDIN' MY TIME

from *Girl Crazy*

Music and Lyrics by George Gershwin and Ira Gershwin

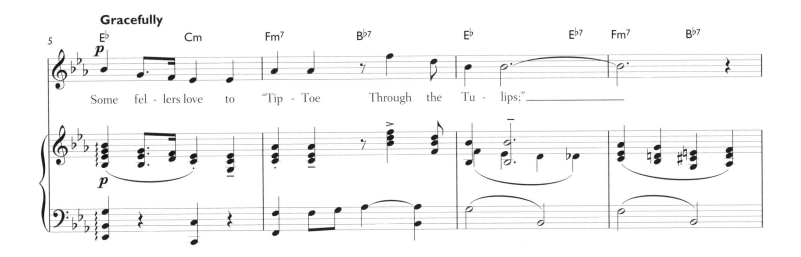

Some fel-lers love to "Tip - Toe Through the Tu - lips;"_____

Some fel-lers go on "Sing - - ing In The Rain."_____

LET'S CALL THE WHOLE THING OFF

from *Shall We Dance?*

Music and Lyrics by George Gershwin and Ira Gershwin
Arranged by Jack Gibbons

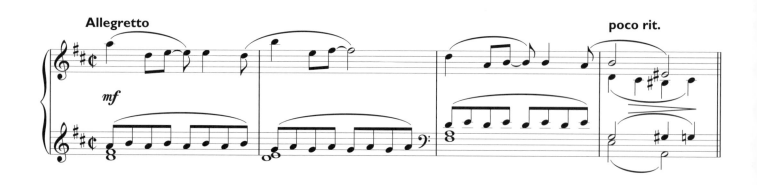

Things have come to a pret-ty pass,___ Our ro-mance is grow-ing

flat, For you like this and the oth-er___ While

174

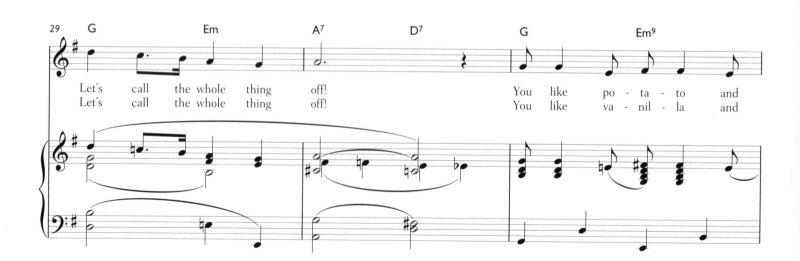

OH, LADY, BE GOOD!

from *Lady, Be Good!*

Music and Lyrics by George Gershwin and Ira Gershwin

SLAP THAT BASS

From *Shall We Dance?*

Music and Lyrics by George Gershwin and Ira Gershwin

Zoom - zoom! zoom - zoom! The world is in a mess! With

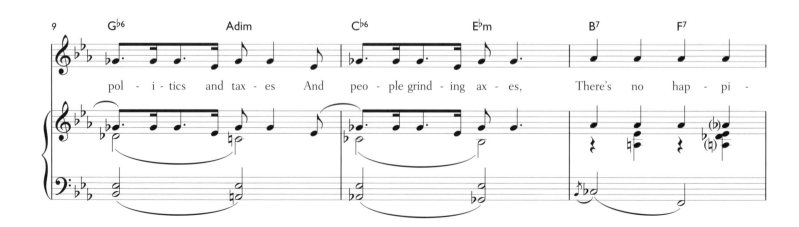

pol - i - tics and tax - es And peo - ple grind-ing ax - es, There's no hap - pi -

SUMMERTIME
from *Porgy And Bess*®

Music and Lyrics by George Gershwin, Du Bose and Dorothy Heyward and Ira Gershwin

186

SWANEE

from *Capitol Revue*

Words by Irving Caesar
Music by George Gershwin

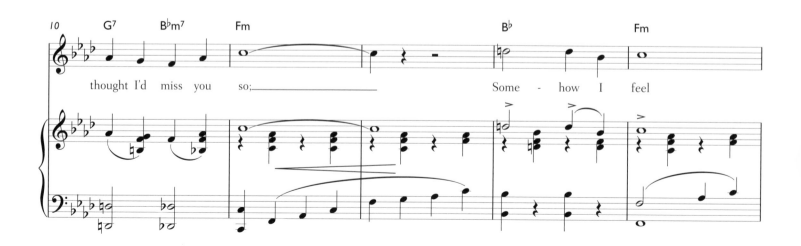

THAT CERTAIN FEELING
from *Tip-Toes*

Music and Lyrics by George Gershwin and Ira Gershwin

194

THEY ALL LAUGHED

from *Shall We Dance?*

Music and Lyrics by George Gershwin and Ira Gershwin

Moderato (gracefully)

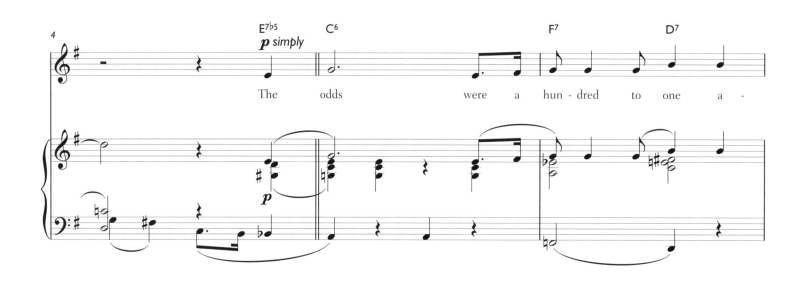

The odds were a hun-dred to one a-

-gainst me. The world thought the

MINE

Music and Lyrics by George Gershwin and Ira Gershwin

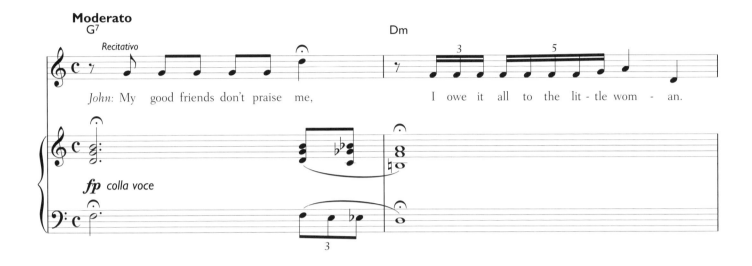

THE HALF OF IT, DEARIE BLUES

from *Lady, Be Good!*

Music and Lyrics by George Gershwin and Ira Gershwin

209

BY STRAUSS
from *The Show Is On*

Music and Lyrics by George Gershwin and Ira Gershwin

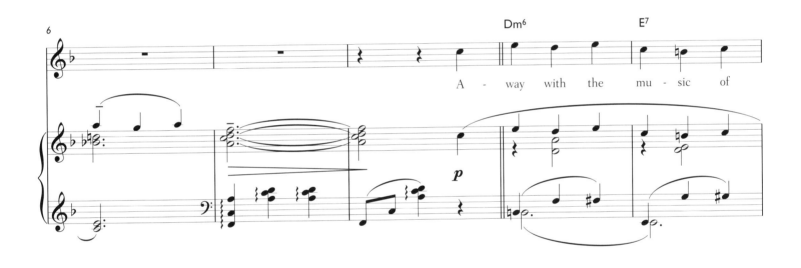

A - way with the mu - sic of

Broad - way!_____ Be off with your Irv - ing Ber - lin!_____